Disney · PIXAR

TOY STORY

**BOOK 9
Long -o**

The Best Cowpoke

ISBN: 978-1-338-57292-6

10 9 8 7 6 5 4 3 2 1   19 20 21 22 23

Printed in Malaysia   106

First printing, 2019

Book design by Marissa Asuncion

Scholastic Inc.

Jessie and Woody
are taking a **stroll**,
when the wind **blows**
Jessie's hat off her head!

Woody **knows**
how to get it down.

Woody gets the **crows**
to knock down Jessie's hat.

"Thanks, Woody,"
says Jessie.

"It's my job
to take care of **folks**,"
says Woody.

Jessie did not like
Woody's **tone**.

"I **know** how
to take care of myself,"
says Jessie.

Woody laughs.
"You couldn't **rope**
your **own** hat
off a cactus," he says.

Jessie did not like
Woody's **joke**.

"I'll **show** you
who is the best cowpoke,"
says Jessie.

The Prospector walks up.
"Now, **hold** on," he says.
"What you need is a
showdown to see who
is the best cowpoke."

The Prospector tells Jessie
she has to **show** a horse
a new trick.

Jessie tries,
but the horse will not **go**.
He is a **no**-trick **pony**!

The Prospector
tells Woody he has to ride
a bull called Old Diablo.

Woody tries,
but the bull will not **go**.
He just wants to
doze in the sun.

Just then, Woody and Jessie
hear a loud *moo*.
A calf is in the river!
It needs their help!

Jessie **throws** a **rope**.
She **lassoes** the calf.
Woody helps **tow** it in.

Woody and Jessie
save the calf!
They are **both**
great cowpokes.